Missy Church's po[ems are] alive with images both [...] their intricacies time and [...]

— William Taylor Jr.

Effervescent and ethereal. Take communion with CHURCH on the toilet, in the bath, while traipsing naked through haunted woods, sliding through slimy kelp forests. Church's words remain like motherly heartburn, the soothing balm of amniotic fluid. One cannot be done, one cannot put down. Once in, Church remains. When lonely, Church's words extend pulp-ridden prognostication of the human condition and rock the reader to sleep at a speed slightly off kilter but ever-so-right.
— JK Fowler

Think of stepping into the Mütter Museum of human emotion. Missy Church's work is a hushed excavation of the marrow of mundane life. Think of taxidermy of soul, a truth telling that turns would-be waste into art, "Poetry is like diarrhea. Once it starts, all you can do is sit and wait it out." The poems in this collection, recollection are reminders of what we already know, but like all bad children, we need to be told again and again. How sublime our sins when we are willing to put them on display. How beautiful, "slit slashes/a worn woman separated/at the mid-line." Church's words cut us open where we might remember from our dusty places that we were "rising from what was once/a wet hot peach" and that here, strangely enchanted words are waiting to take us there again.
— M.k. Chavez

CHURCH grants us insight into the recurring symbols that make up Missy Church's poetry: bodily wounds, domesticity, mental illness, desire, and motherhood. These poems leave raw imprints on the senses reminiscent of Burke's concept of the sublime. Church's poems are solidly constructed with obscene mines placed among the stanzas not to shock, but rather to surprise us into feeling more intensely than is normally sanctioned, to make that affective connection that transforms poetry into a transcendent force in the everyday world. The poems in CHURCH are not for the faint-hearted, yet they resound with a darkly comic personal vision that easily translates into a vision of our daily lives: brutal, sometimes ludicrous, despairing, yet always hopeful.
— Anthony C. Cooke

CHURCH
RETROSPECTIVE

Missy Church Bible

PRESENTED TO
Conner Jones ♥

You sir, are always a piece of our hearts ♥. See you on your death bed... in a nice way ♥

BY **Mrs. Misery Freakazoid Incarnate**

Missy Church

DATE **October 1, 2016**

♥ Corner Jones ♥

CHURCH
RETROSPECTIVE

Old and New Writings

IN HER

Royal Lowness Vision

TRANSLATED OUT OF THE ORIGINAL TONGUES
AND WITH PREVIOUS TRANSLATIONS
DILIGENTLY COMPARED AND REVISED

SELF-PRONOUNCING

CHURCH Retrospective
Missy Church © 2015

All poems herein are the property of Missy Church. No reprints permitted, in part or in whole, without prior consent of the author.

Some of these poems were previously published in *Obscure, Damaged Beyond Recognition, Gathering Of The Minds, Sparkle & Blink, The Lost Frames Compendium,* and *Oakland Review*

Paul Corman Roberts – Associate Editor
Editor, artwork, and print design by Youssef Alaoui-Fdili
Paper Press Books & Assoc. Publishing Co.

ISBN 10 1514664194
ISBN 13 978-1514664193

A   P A P E R   P R E S S

B O O K

For Al and Candy

MISSY CHURCH
RETROSPECTIVE

Paper Press

CONTENTS

Foreword - xv

No. 20
One - 3
Pickled - 4
November Leaves - 6
My Father - 7
Want - 8
Canvas - 9
Cover Charge - 10
Glossary - 11

Unflushed
Adultery - 15
Liquid Religion - 16
580 - 18
Tucson - 20
Watering Slugs - 21
Spin - 22
Laying Light - 24
Jack - 25

Ten - 26
Stranger In My Morning - 28
Air - 29
Between - 30
Vinyl - 31
Everyone Shits - 33
SoCal - 34
L.A. - 36
Listen - 37
Lawrence - 39
80 East - 40
Bound - 41
Sunday P.M. - 44
Monday A.M. - 45
Monday P.M. - 46

Deluxe
Boots - 53
Crow Feet - 54
All American Abortion - 55
Not Enough - 57
Thief - 60
Piles Of Poetry - 61
Deaf - 63
Exposed - 65
Low Tide - 67
I Have Become A Stalker - 70
The Annex - 75

Since
Since - 107
After Birth - 108
This Is Only A Recording - 111
Flowers For The Undead - 113
Three A.M. And Money Is Scarce - 114
Minor Pioneers - 116
Early Days - 118
Alone - 119
An Expectant Sacrifice - 121
Wreckage - 122
What It Takes To Die - 124
I Stitch My Eyelids Together At Night - 126
Thick Ghosts - 128
Losing Streak - 129
Pennies For My Natives - 130
Maternity Leave - 132
The Ramp - 133
Fear Of Time - 135
The Last Song To Be Played At My Funeral - 136

Naked
Birthday Poem - 141
The Abundant Affliction - 143
Bedding Down With A City - 146
Mojave - 148
Morro Bay - 149
Don't Take It Home - 151

Trouble - 153
Oakland - 155
Naked In A Morgue - 158
Popularity - 160
San Francisco - 161

FOREWORD

What is *normal?* What is *dysfunctional?*

Many of our literary gatekeepers, particularly in the poetry world, have come to regret the ascension of the transgressive narrative over the lyrical, but isn't it really a natural progression for the form? Make no mistake, Sylvia Plath and Anne Sexton are not simply the godmothers of modern Goth poetry, they directly impacted the weight and sound of the words that would be used in a great deal of Western poetry, literature, and speech to follow.

If poetry, like punk rock, has become the most democratic form of its medium, based on accessibility, then dark, confessional prose is essentially its grungy, death metal cousin. It's a form grasped for sooner rather than later by the novice who, still coming to terms with their modes of exploration, finds the path of clever deconstruction the least resistant, and most exhilarating, over the exhaustive process of building a model that is capable of building on itself. In other words, yes of course there is a lot of shitty confessional poetry out there. There is also lots of shitty slam poetry, lots of shitty language poetry, lots of shitty new age lyric poetry, and lots of shitty plainsong.

But the confessional form, when it works, is every bit as transcendent as the most seductive of lyric, because it seeks transformation perhaps more aggressively than other genres or forms; because it is more desperate. It is in fact the most potently modern of all poetic forms because it has no patience. It wants to tear it all down and it wants to tear it all down now.

And when this is the sole point of the confessional form, is when it is at its most boring. At its best, it has already moved on from the depths and is striving to build human relationships that are recognizable and infused with some kind of meaning.

This is why Missy Church's poetry goes above and beyond the genre. It is not just another long slow crash down some pre-formulated nihilism, but instead a rhythmic dispatch from a *Generation X*'er forced to stare down her mortality, her parenthood, and her damage from growing up in a disassociated family in a repressed society, eyes wide and unflinching, even as tears stream unchecked down her dark passages.

At some point the form cries out for survivors, for answers, and if not answers, at least a starting point toward moving toward survivors. When we are not in a state of decay, we are in a state of growth. There is no such thing as normal. Therefore there is no such thing as *dysfunctional*. There is only survival; the survival of the body, the heart and the mind working together. Think of it as a new kind of prayer, for which this book offers verses and incantations, much like a bible for this new mode of psychic existence.

Missy Church is quite familiar with both modes. As the next generation of hardened, jaded youth get ready to make that leap from the cauldron of death, they will find Church and her canon waiting for them there, saying *this is how you survive*. Her brilliance is that it is not just young aspiring writers who can learn these survival lessons from her; it is for all of us.

– Paul Corman - Roberts

EDITOR'S NOTE

This selection of Missy Church's poetry, covering the past 20 years of her life, falls under a category usually reserved for visual artists, called *retrospective*. Here the poems are arranged in chronological order with special attention to pieces that best reflect the artist's core intent and follow the trajectory of her career to date.

In addition, the book design is modeled after Missy's great-grandmother's bible, handed down to her when she was a girl. We hope this book will be a pleasure to hold, to roam, and also to provide a valuable resource for those interested in Missy Church's work and her perspective on early love, the passing of her father, meeting her husband, and the birth of her child.

twenty

No. 20

One

I have become convenient
and exact with
the sword of madness
sheathing us behind curtain twitches
me and she
the crazy lady across the street
who postures as a ballerina
on rainy days
balanced on the edge
of porch and publicity

I record her drastic movements
She extends her arms and palms
heaven ward
eyes closed, pursed lips
silken shoes soiled turning wet worms
into chunky beige paste
the ball of her twisting poses
I waste ink and anti-depressants

The rain rouses
tattoos and scars
her curtain of flesh
whose weight is drawn aside
to release the dark
under sheets of rain

I forget to take my medication

Pickled

Glass containers
line my kitchen shelves
a tick-tock rattling
of pacific plate tides

I drink from leaves
drowning in whiskey
and dine on jars
of blank calendar squares

Plush skin forms
along the inside of the jars
quivering in veins of gelatin
the ice of my deeds

A broken seal is remorse
gas popping in thickness
when I come home with the
smell of night

Poised and squat,
I straddle over the
culmination of my doings
chin dripping with gravy

I am the sin pickler
taught and scrawny
bearing the full weight
of bedtime fruit

November Leaves

He pulls from his chest
a nest
of sinewy strands
and brown clumps
exorcised and mistaken
for unfertilized soil

He pours the warm, sloppy mess
from palm to palm
with a blank stare
from his one good eye

He is distant and pointless
a crisp blue sky for a backdrop
of moods that are filtered and burglarized
from neighboring boxes, cardboard
stiff under the snapping sun

He eats his grief from paper plates
with lips that are November leaves
ending up in the gutter
with last week's obituary

My Father

When I arrived
he was asleep
he said he heard me cough
and it woke him up
his legs wobbled underneath him
like busted pick-up sticks
he fell to the floor
in a humid symphony
grasping for his infant cane

Want

There is a man who is
more dead than alive

he slouches
tipped over the sewer scale
like a skeleton sack

we step over his river of urine
it babbles from under
his darkening pants

he is mouthing communications
as natural as a tulip

a hungry fighting bird
lips separated and careless
a want and nothing more

Canvas

It begins
when everyone is asleep
even the mice

I train my hands
to bait the will
into coming
will is not fickle
will is determined
and rarely lets me down
she is trained to slice my leg
from my body
clean

My guppy rolls aside
revealing a fresh canvas
unspoiled for the baby blade
whose edges feel fine
quick
smart
and new

Cover Charge

Death knows no time
illness has no schedule
in these self-fulfilling prophesies
are placed models of lands
and deities and nirvanas
that stand alone as
the last outpost of safety
in regretful malfunction

I am reaching nirvana
by default
and claiming that I
am not fit for life on earth
the lucky ones get a glimpse
and forget

If there really is a jesus
she left town a week ago
on the party train to hell
with everything but you and me and
the handful of sinners
who lost their "get into heaven free" card

GLOSSARY

<u>Cringe</u>- the action of closing myself to the possibility of reality.

<u>Blind Silence</u>- your stare when I think you may hit me if you were a fuck of a man.

<u>Splattering</u>- the sound of the last moment of childhood.

<u>Guppy</u>- the fat roll between my shirt and pant line.

<u>Humid</u>- a family reunion.

<u>Poppy</u>- my love for you, relinquished.

<u>Hurdled</u>- a knowing of completion.

<u>Nine</u>- nine times out of ten, I pretend that it is you.

<u>A Creature</u>- you. never there. only in my mind.

<u>Convolution</u>- the willing desire to destroy ones' self preservation back stock.

UNFLUSHED

zymosis

Adultery

ship bank white pants
revealing fleshy rocking
on columbus' wooden boat
in the harbor of a town
with love no bigger than the sidewalk
and a jesus christ milking
his mid-life crisis
riding hard into the summer
with flowing back
long bristled hair
longing for evil and sin and
to become a mortal man
who cries and fucks
and beats his head
against the steering wheel
of mid day traffic
praying for death

Liquid Religion

The neon cross outside my apartment window
turns from pink to white to pink again
slowly spinning like a drunk

The toilet lid at my back
is the only physical line
supporting my body

I've become a freckled fish
fisting a bottle
like jesus christ
riding the base of a pink beacon
on a dark and sullen street

Liquid fingers curl around me
contradiction like a child
with sex
playfully extending
her moistened palm
wrist pressed against my lips
fingertips wash away my sight
replacing vision with
glassy eyes of denial

Gripping her white shoulders
I drink holy water by the liter
her liquid fingers curl around me
wrist pressed against my lips
fingers cupping my ear
whispering

580

It has been a week and two days
since I closed my perception
to the sound of beating drums
an ocean conjured up by the best
last details I can recall before the crash

With meticulous molecular jerks
I part my eyelids to
reveal the sun setting comfortably
in another's dusk
curls of smoke free themselves
to live and mingle with the sound of city and car

I cannot tell the difference between
screaming brakes and the grinding gasps
that escape my unsteady breath

I cannot feel the difference between
the wind iced tears and
blood melting from my nose
five-eighty south heightens the intensity
of the fluids pouring into my hands
drying like old cake in the creases
creating a velcro sound as
I spread my fingers apart

Garden hose veins fall loose
from my flesh like warm monkey bread
soiling the ruddy transition
from beginning to end

Details intertwine
like seconds into minutes
only the minutes are days in length
stretching before me like a bad book
with a failing plot and weak coffee

Only this is not a book
it is life in all of its misfortunes
setting as my trust into
the fine line of a Britfish
who gouged my aorta
with the blade of his obsessive pen

Tucson

As pale and soft as worn money
the future breathes against my brow
lingering just so
out of reach
on the edge
of tomorrow's horizon

Quietly I tiptoe onto the freeway
headed west with my blood and shoes
dangling in a knot of veins
and soul set against the cast of night

Trails crossing at roadways lost
maps flying at high speeds
out the shattered rear window

Flopping with dead fish
kicked up from
the underbelly of delicate dreams
dust exhaust and stubbed cigarettes

Watering Slugs

Soil
upturned and
black
flecks of deep ill-green
anoint sparkling slugs
groaning for deliverance

Their bellies gape in
an orifice closing
and opening with
a puckered ripping wet-pop
like the sound of my tongue
against the roof of my mouth
attempting to dismantle
a tasteless wafer

Before the priest realizes
that the body of christ
is glued to the roof of my mouth
with a saliva as potent
as the undertow of
a whiskey slug
trying to rid itself
of the body of a nameless god

Spin

Sirens scream
a lonely love maker
drilling up and down before
the climax of singularity
hits a high pitched volume
then speeds and repeats
riding with the rhythm
of the washing machine
tucked tidily under the stairs

Fists reach down
curving the corners
of baby flesh browned
soiled and gutted

Worms turn through fingers
like plastic gum-ball rings
their sooty hearts pounding
all in time with the machine
and the lonely love maker
pressing passionately
into my void

The spin cycle mounts
upon soggy lifeless clothing
disregarding starch whites
riding the rust and shade

of hand and fist
grasping up and down
sweating morbid gravy
against the fine line
between amnesia and reality

With a final surge
of electricity
the cord retracts
from the limp wall

I could feel my last breaths
there were two and then only one
it didn't hurt and then I remember thinking
"this final breath is something amazing"

Clothes fall from the basin
fingers release their grasp
sticky limp arms
where live flesh
once pulsed
now dead

The laundry is done

Laying Light

Bulbs flick alight
start signals
at the inception
of a cosmic drag

Eyes fall down
from a wire train
of yellow lights
strewn across
milk skin
that digs
rivers and waves
as lines converge
into a place where
you succumb
your fragile self to
satellites and solar burn

Go
spend your nights
floating out of bed
slipping about dreams
fueled
by twitching mouths
leaking with acrid juice

Jack

Jetting into an unseen province
lined with a silt of hair
shaken from waking
from a captured dream

A world set off by blue
an open mouthed sky
dotted with cottony dreams
and a dappled silence
fit only for death

Conscious movements ripple
past sandbars of skin
bleached by milk overflowing
and freezing in a zenith of
senses and sunlight

Kale water drawn close
by the geography of culmination
created under fleshy continents
as if something electrically new
engulfs the edges of a second

Ten

The sun beats hot
on a scrotum called El Paso

She is a dry pool of
leftovers
fragrant brides
greyhound buses
British luggage
all left behind together
in a southern draft

Flat empty air circles
the tube of a derelict television
smashed
it sits politely on the curb
undisturbed by the wind
that blows with a low hum
past an alien visitor
who sits as blank
as the white canvas
of a confused painter

Arid cemeteries
cake silver bones that
separate from fertile flesh
and rot quietly
against the crumbling soil

a corpse cradled
in a long winter's nap
its disoriented flanges
stretch for water
at the edge of the map
where my finger trances
a blue line called "ten"

Once
searching for a soul
I ran from coast to coast
my spine stretched
along the interstates
only to end up
in a sweaty corner of Texas
where Brit luggage
and bony fingers
dig at the heat of disaster

Stranger In My Morning

The sheet around my body
binds me like a lie
that squeezes from my
second hand thighs where
cotton fibers dig and
sink into my pores
filling the spaces
where ambiguity ran rampant
while balancing
on a dusted line that
separates the concentrate
forcing the mix of a bad choice

Between the bed blanket
and sweaty dreams
the daylight hour
twists through my hair
wrapping down over my head
my arms and neck
and the sun extracts a truth
that shelters me in sleep as
a billboard of denial
a temple of blindness
a blood of forgetting

Air

The seatbelt light beaming 'on' now for over ten minutes, beckoned me to stand. A flight attendant reminded me of my passengerial duties with a polite statement of fact, "We have landed ma'am – Grand Rapids." Home again. Was it a holiday? An emergency? I had forgotten already.

I sat in my plane seat, still buckled – letting the chasm between standers and sitters widen like the canyon between my brother and me. Our relationship had spread silently and unceremoniously, like the thighs of a whore. One man flinched as his overhead baggage had shifted during flight and threatened a turn of fate. He caught my eye as he regained his balance. He smiled a warm-stranger smile, the kind without attachment. I saw my brother there. In the corner of his smile, grinning in secret on Christmas Eve, stalking Santa. So many words in a single smile.

Time packs the past away with acrid mothballs and outgrown baby clothes. It is something creeping. It is in the absence of words. It is indefinable moments like this, left to untangle on the flight out of town.

Between

Morning tree branches
pick at my hair
untangling the dreams
still hot with sleep

Limbs stretch for the alarm
heaving deep within
milky dark promises
of slumber

Lunar beams trace
a path under the bed
sheet wrapped tight
against the pitch

Leaves dig deeper
knotting my night brain
with the waking scream
of night nesting birds

Open beaked and wild
talons tear at threads
binding fertile foliage
to the slate of another day

Vinyl

I think I feel
something dying inside me
it stretches its glittery self
from my scalp to my genitals
and out with a slip
resting easily on
the black vinyl
beneath me
in this stale coffee house

Unlike myself
it is unbiased and vibrates
alone, left to dry as
a nugget of wisdom
might lodge its gentle self
for a destined future or
an anonymous poem:

"The zen of black vinyl is
colorless and odorless
disguising its previous guest
with an invisible grin"

My glittery ancestors
glide upon its slick skin
our uterine home bleeds
with the knowledge

of a faceless eternity
where a door opens
to a house of no words

For we are immortal
and you are a container
breeding us to life
with no trace
of our life or death

Everyone Shits

.My bowels are those of a sea sponge, absorbing life indiscriminately.

.Fog is a cotton finger that spreads an icy infection releasing the melancholy of indifference.

.My body paints a portrait of caramel on the reflective canvas between my thighs.

.Poetry is diarrhea. Once it starts, all you can do is sit and wait it out.

.Coconut milk cocktails rule!

.Philosophy and poetry are old men with a lot to say when no one will listen.

.I have been smacked by the frozen, de-mittened hand of Michigan.

.The absence of thought lingers loudly.

.Death always knocks, but only once.

.The universe is listening. So are my neighbors.

SoCal

Stones Boulders Pebbles
become the unknown
lizards mountain lions beetles
moving in the corner of my eye
sand kicked up
from tight-lipped sandals
the drum beat
leading us through the desert

Hail!
Desert madness
when the body is
only head and feet
encased in hot air
and the wind like foam
warm comfort kissing
red golden skin
whispers home

Calling through desert palm
and agave graveyards
rattle those century old stalks
throwing death to heaven

Somewhere between
the whipping
the rattling

the rushing
she calls my name
faint like a faery sneeze
under the radar of busy fears

And yet you know you are desert-mad
when the breath you take
catches on the sight of a boulder
as the names come
in the wilds of the secret dry wind
with hot on her lips
matching the drumming mantra
in the sole of my feet

L.A.

In the backseat of L.A.
stories roll off the sheets
their chunky details of gravel
dig in like a twisted channel
at the end of the TV guide

The old Hollywood is still alive
held together in the photos and tales
of Mrs. Howell and her lady friends
spread like a thick paste
over leathery hills
where young Moriarty comes to chat
on Saturday afternoons

She prefers that the gentleman
prepare the drinks
he mixes three Tom Collins
and one stiff gin and tonic

This blazing tale
of an old world comet
is running out of sky

They are horsed messengers
keeping the longest tails alive
in the unkempt dark
of a new world Hollywood

Listen

'My Own Messiah'
fucks one another
in the summer winds
of a town called Spring Lake

Two boys stroke the strings
of their unplanned future
one wails in my ear
while I close my eyes
and remember
a virgin birth rising
from soiled sheets

Jason bellows –
"Jesus likes his broads with a good ass…"
he rolls around inside his head
eyes closed, plucking his lips
singing "I hate this townnnn…"

A thousand miles away
my uncle stares
star-ward
alone
rotting with blemish
on the border of Mexico –
one eye in the socket
the other in a barrel

In Derek's living room
Listening to Jason
I think
'Yeah, I hate this town too'

Lawrence

The wrinkles in your face
carve a map
unmatched by
the silk of your smile
a transcendental instruction vessel
carries you from bed
to street to store to stage
and bed again

I wonder what your dreams are iced with

The deep lines in your forehead relax
under San Francisco's full moon show
playing center stage night after night
connecting your thoughts
your spilled poetry running alone
in the wide worded desert
that bakes with phrase
and history

Your face will never change
in the constant winds
of your voiceless open sky
You are history

80 East

Golden breasts rise
with heaving oily lust

Worms roll
in sunny desire
under California sun

Here her thighs spread
as shores of passion
well up from the inside
of caramel flesh
pimpled with pines
like a toy train town
before a Maxfield
pink painted sunset

Bound

My fingers are torn
from the taught
of burgundy purple
in the ribbons
around my wrists

They bind me
to the trays
of tepid food
shoveled into my mouth
at a dollar a bite

I am forced to eat
this way for months

My eyes are focused
and pinned open
staring at the false god
of perfection

My mouth
is permanently shaped
in the grotesque form
of a wall clock

My tongue
ticking

my lips ever open
to accept the sacrament
of a divine plan

The ribbons
The food
The plans
fondle my calm
with chaos

As I pee in my apartment toilet
the door closed this time
as an escapee
from the other room
is sprawled
like a trailer park tornado

Vomit in shades of blood
hair hanging through fingers
sobs drowned out
by guests
all the fucking guests

Whatever it is
I once had
is gone
and the only ones
who can save me now
are the Buddhists
heads shaven of all regret
earthen bodies stripped down
to gold tunics

void of ribbons
plastic forks
and wedding guests

They carry me away
sobbing into the vacuum desert
across oceans and
up the slope of a blonde hill

My ribbons
and cuts
and feces
and guests
evaporate into
the dry of the breeze
light and warm
skin brittle plastic

My tattoos and moles
turn into birds and mosquitoes
until all that is left of me
is flesh
suspended
above shaven heads

Sunday P.M.

It is Sunday night

Drinking the last of
the wedding whiskey
watching 'Footloose'
I think Kevin Bacon
has just got to be
someone's hero

I am lonely
deep in the caverns of marriage
that feeling of crying all day
without shedding a tear

Monday A.M.

Eyes
lips
reflecting
with a rainbow iridescence
on a glazed over Monday morning
writing and driving again

Leonard lets me in once more
into his finely padded home
solid in olive green and grays
somewhere in the wheaten countryside
tucked in for the day with sky solid rain

I offer up my body
like a good catholic
to her horny christ
my eyes looking back at me
from the heavy door knocker
hung on Leonard's salty door

Monday P.M.

My body is exhausted
and the June bug
who works the counter
at the corner store
of caffeine and poetry
has come smashing down
into my forehead

She flies without
direction or care
I have no currency
to offer in exchange
for one strong cup of
worthwhile stanza

all sound y...
every rain pu...
the smeared sp...
the hot piss of...

...y into
...misty...
...the light of...

DELUXE

.there.

Boots

The sun dips down
pursing his fiery lips
upon the business
of someone else's day

My big black boots
hang sturdy on me
like tiger teeth
solid in the gums
of a gentle and quiet beast

Midwest clouds
soft over the city tonight
I watch the obedient
trailing flocks
of military rows pinched off
from the bellowing night

Crow Feet

The sunset spills
across my desk and lately
smells like a mid life crisis

Colors slink through
my books pens paper
claws like a foul stench

Dusky rainbows of fault
light upon my
orange belly fat

Crimson memory loss and
indigo knee cramps
this raven of age and time

Clutches tight to
the shadows of inevitable
knowing and denial

Twilight cowers
behind a never ending tide
of blackening dye

All American Abortion
Sister Poem to *Watering Slugs*

> Like a slug that moves along in slime,
> like a woman's miscarried child.
> They will not see the sun.
> – Psalm 58:8

The soil of my sin
is upturned and black
sort of letting out from
confessional convictions
a demented chalice of holy water
anointing the greasy slugs
that groan and suckle for deliverance
at my blood flecked toes

Their mouths smack open
puckering with a
rip. wet. pop.
echoing the sound of my tongue
digging at the roof of my mouth
in an attempt to dismantle
a tasteless wafer
delicately sliced
from the flesh of somebody's jesus
placed in my mouth

My tongue prods secretly
before the priest realizes
that yes. indeed.

the body of christ is now
stuck to the roof of my mouth
with a saliva as potent as the underbelly
of the slug that now inches its way
from my holy place
dribbling wet with regret

In the name of the father
and the son and
the holy ghost
it's fucking stuck
conformed to my palate
with a mind of its own
like an immaculate conception
occurred behind my pursed lips

The glossy slug works its way
down my thigh
moist with want
the wafer loosens its pasty self and
flakes of god's sacrament
slide down my throat
I gulp and fight the groan
rising from my bleak and raw belly

Not Enough

I've been carrying this grudge
of a poem for days now
on the N-Judah
the 47
the J
and home again

Sleep and repeat

I have switched from
wine to whiskey
medium to large
hangers to vibrator
cash to credit
stripes to solids

And
only after losing six games
of American pool
to my British husband
do I find my pen
furious enough
to kick the ass of
this piece I began last week

in an attempt to
exorcise you from me

It is
Thursday night and
my penmanship tells me
that I am drunk

It is only 6.30
the swell of ominous fog
outside my window
pushes me deeper
into my head
the words I write
are forcibly illegible
and congeal into a crude portrait
of your lustful body

My eyes have been stripped
down to blighted walls,
the rods and cones
blink intermittently like
cheap Christmas lights

I see only in colors of
anger and envy
since I let you touch me

where I bleed
in an unchristian sort of way

I hate myself
for getting this wrecked
on a school night
forgetting birthdays and
killing that possum when
I was twelve years old
and for buying into one sided love

I hate myself
but not enough
to ever fuck you again

Thief

My sight has been stripped bare
down to the rods and cums
the Christmas colors of
loss and regret
fuck and forget
pre-treat and launder
write and repeat

I steal lines from
plucked poems
like a lovers mask
that is becoming
soiled with repeat offenses
my corneas blighted
I walk Van Ness and inebriation
the fog of our alleyways
and the late night blood lettings
litter the trail behind me

A zombie
a lingering ghost boy
of our love
walked twice and spat upon
stuffed with shredded filings
of your tossed writings
wasted ejaculations
festering in the palm of
our unfinished business

Piles Of Poetry

the innocent child is not skeptical
and bites the heads of young crisp stems
daisies are best
they are rotten with innocence

i walk and drink in the night
as a strand of my hair breaks free
and swims...

he rolls his sorrow
between the fingers
of his unfortunate loneliness
he is the child
I will never bear

my naked feet step upon the pages
of his delicately written poetry
untouched like silver looking glasses
like rolling dew just before dawn
in a forest we once roamed
in that other life before
creatures made the tic-tock clocks

this carpet is a canvas
of unfortunate accounts
one pile for the right foot
one for the left

two night slippers
literate support for my toes
shuffling sole bound podiatrists
searching for that soft spot
where my fingers dig tenderly
one more death

but this is the fear
in the poverty of friends
as I await another ambulance
to drag the leaking carcass away

Deaf

*A poem for reading after eight years of silence
and gratitude to the one who festered inside of me*

He has been living
in my head
for so long now
that the stench
of his flesh
has begun to harden

Over my lips and nostrils
crusting the folds of my brain
rendering me into
an altered state of mobility

The odor is not a mucus
nor a pus
but more of a
thick dessert cake
gone fungal on the tongue
like my desire

The air of this decomposition
in mildewed condensation
is a seething swollen tick
suckling on the sewage
of my intellect

One night, this beast
will cave in upon itself
releasing odious desires
on my barren heart
crusted with grisly memory
and unshaven organs

Exposed

The ghost of your arms around me
the sidewalk outside my bedroom
a stripped and pulsing wound
open crimson waves
flash in the setting sun
caught between the fronds
of curling palms
the fight for survival
of your memory

You have become the face of
everyone I am not supposed to love
and if I were free I
would find you and fuck you
on the map that I draw daily
with a switchblade
on my thigh
lead way with bread crumbs
to the steps of your home

If I were free
I'd do what I was told
in the old fashioned way
with a clump of my hair
in your fist and we'd fight
fucking me as the traffic backs up
outside your window

under the blackened leaves
I collect from the sidewalk below and
press into my book.

Low Tide

I search for your scent
in this corner bar
like a delusional bloodhound
I sip cold wine and try to bleed out
the 90's bar music with my headphones

At the end of Wicked Game
(by Chris Isaac)
wafting between barstools
I feel your phantom fingers
press into my arm
my cellular memory puckers
at the thought of your flesh against mine
where you sliced me, in ceremony
and medicated me with cheap wine and promises

(I cover the scar with a tattoo now, and call it good)

The hair in my lips tastes
like tannins and you
our tongues held the memory of a magic
we kept secret in the glitter I spread
on your porch
my desperate calling card
for months at a stretch
until your jealous tantrum
and I went back to my little life

I am ridiculous and foolish
and no better than you
to come stalking around your home
like a desperate ghost
looking for closure
our city a graveyard
of ghosts with bleached teeth
gummed by loss, potions and pavement

I calculate time
in the margins of a notebook
since we last spoke:
it has been two years
three months
twenty-five days

My written words prove desperation
magnified by 4 o' clock cocktails
a half-block from your door
where the wine is bitter
and it only comes white
unlike that old Gallo
and our open veins
diseased with our
rituals wrought
bite and blade

I stammer and gag on memories
we'd become siblings that night
even brothers and sisters fight
and maybe speak to one another on holidays

but I can no longer claim you in my
family tree
her limbs are too heavy

Someone bumped against the jukebox
here at the High Tide Lounge
spilling a sharp mix of AC/DC and wiry static
I want to turn and see you there
smiling at the Rockola
our wicked book in hand
smeared with elixir we'd created by night
like a loaded gun between impulsive bed sheets

The bartender knocks the music
back into submission
I have become
a stalker of disgusting proportions
and have had enough
of your evasive perfume for now

I Have Become
A Stalker Of Disgusting Proportions

I know where you live
I spend my lunch breaks
measuring the empty space between
the you and the me
it is 972 feet

Some days it's more
some days less
depending on my agitation
it takes me 12 minutes there and
15 minutes back, uphill
I savor the three-minute window
as I crouch in the dirty shrubs
at Post and Turk

My desire comes in the afternoon
I savor leftovers of your
digested poetry
that I squirreled away
from our early afternoon dates
outside your urban home

I survive on your poetry for sustenance
for breakfast I eat the poem about
black birds at sunrise
for lunch, I masturbate with a copy of your book

and for dinner I dine on *Eclipse*

Some nights, when sleep does not come
I spread my tongue across
the poem about your corpse
in hopes of ingesting minute crumbs
of your skin
embedded in the valleys of ink and pulp

Hiding inside this bush I
can watch you rise
at noon again
my little second story porn star

You wear
a tight white tee shirt
stained with Gallo
and rise slowly
turn on the computer
inspect your eyes in the mirror
scuttle past the massacre
of the night before
the battlefield litter
empty wine bottles
crumpled paper
and loneliness

Your private life rattles my loins
I dig into my pants
calling to you with my best stalker gaze
summoning desire
my breathing swells

below the view of buses pedestrians and taxis
you pause and lean
over the kitchen sill
to roll a cigarette
my fingers stiffen into myself
watching you place your fingers to your lips
and take a breath
deep enough to display
the want I want
and your despair

I quiver under your divine presence
I brush the city soil from my knees
and huff the nine blocks back to work

.here.

The Annex

I.

(Monday)
I begin another life tomorrow
where adults live

(Tuesday)
Today I became an adult
under the cloud of my
Father's death

Last night I feigned the words
of a speechless beginning

As my Fathers cat, Missy
stepped delicately over
my Dad's juicy head
to piss in her litter

His body lay soiled
by its own inner workings
for forty two hours
on the bathroom floor
in his all-alone home

II.

The second day of his death
the fifth for his body
now casked in a stranger's refrigerator

I awoke with a voice
"Do you have the consciousness to change?"

Words of the dead
floating down into tangible
places that we can accept as real
voices we can hear in life

I take these sounds
my Father's transmissions
pluck them from my tangled hair
and bead them into bracelets
and pieces I can finger
like an old woman's rosary

III.

Words fall from my lips
or so it seems
I speak
echo
stare
did I say something?
I think so
I create a tale

"Pain is best served in large doses"
grates a voice in the silence
it is death
speaking to
his victim's child
playing darkness over
the man splayed out
upon the bathroom tiles

Grey grout soiled brown and red
puckers under the dark of
the reapers shadow

The corners of his cloak
mutate and begin devouring
what lies left of a
mortal man

From the armpits
the dermis is filleted

tender old muscles fall open
wrapped delicately around
my shoulders
from arm to ankle
my father becomes a meaty
feast for the soil

After detailed inspection
eyes
hair
tongue
Death continues his deconstruction
pausing only to slip
his salty tongue
around the black and decomposing
lung

The remainder left
for the undertaker
who will harvest the body
for what can be
trimmed
pinned
photographed
as nicotine damage
liver disease
a broken heart

IV.

Midwest hotel room
I spread my Father's life
across a bed
a museum of regret
it is nearly one a.m.
(only eleven on the west coast)
piles of papers
separated by importance
leaking brown cigarette smoke
and nagging sighs of confusion
outside the wasting summer
bends into September
katydids pop off night songs
they drown the hum of the air conditioner
my father's smoky handwriting
on checks and the backs of envelopes
stare at me from their pile on the floor
he left a tome of paperwork
half a bottle of pills and
a plastic wine glass
empty
unwashed

V.

A week gone
the singing dusk insects
now quiet
in this new season

It is almost four in the afternoon
sitting in my Dad's kitchen chair
rolling across the clicking tiles
I spin like a kid
listing to his classical music
it's getting cold
last week of summer the season
shifts abruptly here
the leaves of Lakeshore have gone
yellow, gold, orange, some red
a venerable Japanese maple looks like
blood fireworks in a weakening sky

I have aged a million years
in these eleven days
school bus stops outside
dad's dwindling house
three children hop out
and disappear
across the street

VI.

The thickness of birch trees
behind my father's house
sway and bring on the autumn wind
sallow leaves
fall and scoot around
the cement patio
otherwise bare
as parallel wooden lovers
racing for the heavens
roll between the fingers
of Midwest wind
nearby the lake

We pulled down his bird feeders
I can imagine the snow
that will stream across his windows
in a few months

Dad's rolling chair
is littered with cigarette burns
it catches on the tiles of the kitchen floor

Most of his home is now emptied
of things I could ever want
or need
for legal reasons
the 'taters' box
next to the shotgun
near the back door

is empty
Missy the cat
and her cat things
left with her on Wednesday
my job is finished

VII.

The first left
off Lake Odessa exit
between Grand Rapids
and Lansing
in a little house
alone on an empty windswept plot
jazz falls from the bedside radio

Dave the hometown boyfriend
is moving things around
in his new home here
making comforting noises
while I sit warm
in the bed
where we used to love

Tonight I said goodbye
to my Father's house
to the man I love
and tomorrow, to a friend
I never knew I had
in San Francisco

VIII.

Had to hand my father's ashes
to a sky porter as I boarded the plane
in Grand Rapids this morning

In a broken voice, tearing up
I asked him to be careful
with the bag

IX.

Grief is an unattractive beast
whose talons tear
into the muscles of the afflicted
its coarse whiskers grasp
at lips, cheeks, and brow
contorting the face
into a bizarre concoction of
the underworld's cruel laughter

X.

Advice regarding
my Fathers death

"Meltdown"
"If you need a little help take a Zanax"
"An hour in the sky and you'll feel better"
"Call the lawyer"
"Call your husband"
"Call your mom"
"Get drunk"
"Write it down"

His body was too decomposed to be displayed
at the memorial
I grasped my eldest aunt's thigh
like a bottle of gin
and wrote about it later that night

Grief is harsh
and bitter like vomit
and it comes up
when I least expect it
I want to get drunk and have an affair
to make myself feel better

XI.

At the time of death
human death
body death
there is nothing to pack
everything physical is left behind
glasses, hats, hair, shoes, tools, rings
watch, eyes, implants, books
cups, couch, socks, broom, shirts, coins, breath

Everything my Father read
spoke, thought, shared, loved
cried, smelled, ate, shit
is now somewhere
somewhere

XII.

Today at 9:20
I cried
on the last paper towel
left in my dad's kitchen
my tears were heavy rocks they
curled into my eyeglasses
like boulders bounding off cliffs

XIII.

When I was a child
I wondered how Santa could find me
if I was at Grandma's house for Christmas

For my Father's death
I was in Philadelphia
an unfamiliar to my Dad
now walking down a street
that he and I walked together
when we went to see
the liberty bell
I was nine

I dream of him every night
trying to sort out the scene
of his home dismantled
and disposed
it must be a nightmare
to watch your world
sifted, sold, and separated
a fucking nightmare

XIV.

My Father
digs through his belongings with me
keep
donate
dump

It's a linear process
free of emotion
we are separate but
agree on the outcome of
meaningless objects made of plastic
wood is good
silver is better
we prepare for his death
along with his twin brother
uncle Elbert
the three of us
sorting our lives

There are oil paintings
mugs, quilts, albums, file folders
smoky papers and
an air freshener in the shape
of a red opaque cat
with a red light on its head

I knew Dad never liked it
but it went into the 'keep' pile
because it was from me

we all smiled
Elbert laughed
and the brown spots
at his temples darkened
under the stress
of having been dead
for so long

I watched the two brothers
rocking in laughter
now bound to decay and mold
in this new world
they move as one

XV.

I am a quiet mourner
one who moves slow and
wants to be left alone
in the din of sorrow

I will never see my Dad again
I am orphaned
in the 'Little Quiet Children's Home'
on the outskirts of this
drizzling city

No amount of candy or money
is going to fix this fucking nightmare
my blood level
mixes nicely with red wine
and I might
have already shut off
from this life

XVI.

My Dad is dead

XVII.

New shoes pound the pain out of me
grief is not like raging weather
a hurricane to be tracked
upon the emotional Doppler
nor is it raging in ridiculous
enormity or red-faced intensity

These are uncontrollable circumstances
that can be pinpointed
splayed out like an amphibian
sunning on the rock
of space and time

XVIII.

I wish
my dad were still alive
for just one more year
without pain
and a fully functioning body

You see, praying
is the foolproof version of wishing
if you give up the control
then there is no fault
wishing does no good
wishing is for amateurs

'Wish in one hand
Shit in the other
See which fills up first'

The planet is round
under my shoes
it no longer holds
the corpse of my father

The rain falls
as fast and hard
as my tears
inside my home
my husband asks
if I need a towel
or a warm drink
or wine

I need a father

XIX.

Crying occurs one drop at a time
unexpected and welcome
I am the executioner
of my father's estate
dried and riddled with
leaves of a corrupted fall
the whip of adulthood
cracks my spine
tearing me down from
memories of you
jags of attention
vie for rank
un mounted
un bridged
blind, raging wild
in a field of despair

XX.

There is a song planted into
the folds of my memory
that will never be the same
it will be on every recording purchased
from this day forward

The tone is set by
my feet lumbering across the floor
"...not at all"
I curse the song
a quitter before beginning
it is a death song
it drives pylon needles
into the beats of my drum
past the anvil and hammer
firmly planting into a
grey covered organ
groaning in the slow-pulsed speak
of a sick woman
on the floor below

The third chorus opens with a growl
of cellos and a bass racing on a steep incline
weaving around one another in a push
for the finish line between
human and rodent
their bodies consuming opposite
quantities of earth
but equal parts of elemental space

salt and pepper
rock and sand
valley and hill
death and life

XXI.

My footfalls are hexed
they deliver Morse code
to angels of death
vibrations trim through
the floor and transmit
a version of this song in wicker
those who are already gone
sing at night now so
I bind my feet in woolen gauze
to shut out the noise
the hosts sing graven tunes
that flow through caverns
in my bones

XXII.

I sleep in the stink of my Fathers habit
and dream my disgusting memories
that never breathed the air of day

I read my Father's books for breakfast
snuggled into the blanket he loved
kept on the couch for serious naps

His belongings fit into a 3x5 box
that fits through my apartment door
the rest broke in the mail

Each breath is expired for him
lost on a Sunday corpse
wrought in despair and ashen thoughts
as the sun sets and rises
in the bed of my father's thumb
(in the bed of the earth)

And today
this becomes a new metaphor
it is the innocence of a child's belief
it is the perfection and innocence
of a father in her eyes
and the perfection
and innocence of magic

It is the love
of this union
at last

.for Sylvia.

Since

Since I was ordered to crawl upon my back
and spread and push and get mad
the empty easy days have been far
and few between my thighs you tried
your little best of an effort
you mighty
piece of perfect flesh
with a crown of blonde
furrowed baby brow
and bud petal lips fishing for air
facing our world out here
will be the greatest
boy scout badge of honor ever sewn
upon your life chest with
my still growing coffin hair
since that night
raining on a ridiculous town
I have put my pieces back
taped them tight enough
to keep what is mine from rusting
the unconditional
gaze you cast upon my face

After Birth

I.

Under the long dark hours of night
you climb upon my body
you filthy uninvited beast
settling into my flesh
in a dust of razor splinters
hurling stars of white pain
onto the ripe folds of my belly

I am neither world
my parts have been severed and sold
for a fetal price
ears agile and adept
bristling hair tines vibrating
at levels fit for
bats and babies

In this new realm of
soft-soled listeners
swirling on a rock
alone, grey-skied, and pocked
with sun slits
like an over used blanket
saddled with holes

II.

My slit slashes
a woman worn and separated
at the mid-line
I will hide it well
stretch marks mar as flames
rising from what was
a hot wet peach

Cuts on my thighs and
nights well spent
hidden between
a deep ethereal muscle memory
will come in time
no longer measured by
months, days, hours, or
Hail Marys whispered without belief
even the fat clock of
regret ticks to the feelings
slowly growing
inside me

III.

Now he is moving in space
wild with spider knowledge
of what I am thinking
of what I am feeling
and hiding

He knows the hues of
my impossible desperation
and fear of motherhood
he knows already
things too human to be soiled
by my dysfunction and loathing

My unfinished business
my desire
a swept floor
never clean
he is a piece of me now
a piece to be pulled out
of my severed trunk
he is brave and pliant
out on his own
lost in a world of dry expectations
a vessel of perfection
pink and wet and
screaming

This Is Only A Recording

Side A-

Morning Sickness:
greedy snatch gremlins
flailing odors of rancid
decomposition

Contractions:
tree in my grip
cars blur by wide rim lake
grasp for dear life

3:41 AM Birth:
"half hour Melissa!"
mining fear with scalpel threats
clock strikes like hell

Recovery:
lizard skin baby
plucked and secreted away
from his former home
called me

Side B-

Morning Sickness:
you are favored here
what a perfect possibility
a growing baby

Contractions:
the moments begin soft
coaxing me into a state
of leaden roots

Birth:
familial supports
holding legs between moments
of dark and exhausted deaths

3:40 AM Recovery:
once around the sun
his cry calls me stumbling
this year I will hold him

Flowers For The Undead

The compulsory flowers of birth
are dying in the water of a vase
red as the blood
that still flows from me
hallmark of unfinished labor
mom leaves today
she arrived a mother
leaves a grandmother
with me caught in the middle
monkey in the middle
middle stack balance
bottles and diapers
fear and doubt
little nose and fingers
terror and stick figly things
poke
into the darkest parts
of my brain
I am on my own

Three A.M. And Money Is Scarce

He sells me
tiny moth breaths
not to be confused with Sylvia's
peanut butter and sandwich son
my child lights the midnight hours
I guess I'm safe
from gas-induced suicide

What will you purchase with
my family currency
with wool socked feet
from his bed to mine
in a dimly lit hallway
with no socket for light
shadows pave the way
from this to that
room of hot
limp bundles

Tearing at the night infused door
a mouth the size of a nickel
his little monetary lips beg
in expectancy for
something

He will never inherit
my disorder

wilting and asleep
my midnight hands lifting his
weightless body to my bed
a soft bedroom haze
bathes the two of us like
the only humans on earth
his breath slows and softens
limp fingers flicker into dreams
stealing this moment
I remember more difficult nights

Minor Pioneers

A wind pushes
the effort of our padded feet
yours exposed to the path
ahead following the sun
winter set spring bound and
pocked with clouds

The gale winds my crooked steps
and trails metered behind your stroller
tired and disheveled I am
your mule-pack guardian
at your service dear Vaughan
and this icy bay whose fingers
lap at our sides
has become a world for birds
crabs and soft-shelled beings

A blur to their lives
the elements here have only begun
to sort us into scientific categories
we minor pioneers sift through
the day still separated by life
bound by the searing of our flesh

The fighting hope
that you do not inherit my disease
I can feel the little beast

creep, creeping in like
a spindly cloud of black needles
fastened to neurons
and other forms of science

Wait, waiting the call of
the relief troops to unlock
thick, thickening of the cave door
but I'll shield you with a sooty wing
and cast a glance
at my pink and naked
my perfect child

Early Days

Three in the afternoon
bright Oakland home
the dryer thumps a
chubby load
intermittent kicks
snaps and zippers metal hot
drum constantly
constantly spins
always in the same direction

I've been drinking earlier these days
a newborn screams in my arms
inconsolable and thumping his
heavy legs against my thighs
to fight his way from my
un-motherly clutch
I sob
and drink to calm us

Alone

The window here
on Park and Encinal
is thick
with old man glass and
silhouette reflections at dusk
multicolored lamps and neon beer signs
pimping out various drinks to
remind me
I may now drink
in solitude
and acceptance

I am alone for the first time
in nine months and 21 days
my body, fully mine now
yesterday went insane
it was suggested to me
by my husband
by my therapist
by my best friend
that I "get out"

Get out of the sobbing operas of mania
get out of the infant cries that drown
what I last knew as normality
get out of the house
get out of depression

get out of house wine
get out of the wreckage
get out of it all
tonight I drink alone

An Expectant Sacrifice

I broke myself open for you
a soft coconut cut stitched up
with the fine glass thread of
doctor 'So and So'
she called it "time"
and the nocturnal animals
that shadowed me
for four continuous days
crept back to their dens to
wait for the next dam to burst

Wreckage

Do you want to fuck me?

Will it be you who takes responsibility for the wreckage
will you peel me of these dirty nightclothes
and fold them along their creases
will it be you who runs your supple fingers along my
thick rough stretch marks swollen with
spent semen still writhing with an empty palm
will you mop up the rivulets of pus
still leaking from my swollen groin which resembles
a palette of undercooked, pounded flesh
that has been sifted through the rusty holes of a meat grinder
will it be you who takes thread to needle and
delicately stitches my angry fascia back together
that throbs beneath a layer of skin that grins
from hip to aching purple hip
will you bind my weeping nipples
clad them down into my breasts with
the subsidized gauze of convention
will it be you who gathers up my regrets like
a wilted bouquet of week old flowery sentiment

Will you scrub away the damage caused by your cock
because this ain't no romantic Titanic waiting to be
resurrected
by weepy eyed scientists looking for a heart of blue
my cunt is a mess and my mind much worse

chunky, bleeding and un-bandageable by the best of 'em
will it be you who pulls me out of this mossy grave

Do you want to fuck me?

What It Takes To Die

Spring came today jumping up and down
like a child on Christmas morning
the air filled with jittering butterflies
fly-fucking in a wicked little dance
their furry sausage bodies writhing
so their wings merge as one
creating a single spiraling eye
under the old pine
in the back yard
my arms window rested
within this chasm
I saw myself –
a ghost reflected
face within face
lips within lips
eye within eye
my iris radiant
and flowing
black green
copper brown
circling spectrums
teasing out the truth
this is the autumn
that holds my desire
it is not the time
it takes to die
it is the time that

drives me out of bed
into the mock of light
that drills my fingers
to write, write, fight.
write or lose it forever
this is the season
that kills me slowly
growing larger by night
over taking my attention
until it blankets
all that I am
under the weight
of so many deaths
it is this that takes me
to my premature grave
deep and stiff under night birds
who are shadowed within
slumbering trees
that copulate
moon warmed mosquitoes
mocking the opposite
drawing us all out
into the wet and dirty open
this is what it takes to die

I Stitch My Eyelids Together At Night

Fastening my eyes
at night
in the dark
has become a risky endeavor
the business of tearing open my face
to the menacing cloak of dawn
brings with it the uncertainty
of my moods
unlike the widower who sees
his love's complexion waning
on the horizon as he draws his drapes aside
to another long and lonely day
marking time across his well worn floors
I read my forecast separate from
the looking glass sky
rap, tap, tapping outside
my bedroom window
the smudge of a sullied, foul ashtray
slamming into the back of my head
slicing brain organ exposed
extracting the disease
shards slicing slowly
bleeding wisps of black-vapors
from an organ labeled depression
searing sting yellow jackets
tabasco-laced barbs
coupled with derelict pockets of fresh

sealed plump bags of blue air
popping between the clouds
heaven's fresh air reserves
sparked with the strychnine of
jitter crusted mania

Or will
the sunrise bring
normality
a killer peppered with
salmon tablets of nothingness
sandwiched between the high and low
roulette wheel spin
mania or depression
during the darkest sour parts of night
I forecast

Thick Ghosts

Depression rises like an ugly scar
dilapidated and sluggish
without regard for my
well thought plans
he is long-limbed slow and thick
he is visible
unreachable and
no broom handle can lodge his funk
he is a drain fucked up with a hair clog of slime
dirty laundry piles
sedation
stuffy heads
dead and rancid
thick tongued fish and
the realization that I
am fucked

Losing Streak

Most of the time
it is piss
not blood
it's blanks
not bullets
it's payouts
not loss
most of the time
the pendulum swings
in the general direction
of luck

It's lost
not found
it's off
not on
it's bad
not good
it's depression
not lithium
most of the time
we're alone
in the company
of others
most of the time

Pennies For My Natives

Tonight I must get back up
on my haunches and
take a look around
it is too late now
for the tired old show
where the last character standing
is a ghost of the person he once was
holding center stage
under a milky yellow
spotlight
glassed with the stagnant dust
of someone caught in the crosshairs

It is too late for these mangy rusty razors
riddled with last night's red stains
bleeding brown the thigh
it is too late to be packing vodka bottles
in the lunchbox each day
sucking the tit at every bus stop
hoping the fresh air of new passengers
will kill the odor of alcoholism
it is too late to be fat
it is too late to drink wine from a box
it is too late to be overmedicated
it is too late to be fucking up

It is too late to be ruining
the fresh flesh of life lips puckered
head extended in infant expectancies
waiting for family history to kick in and
go begging for coins
that we cannot cash

Maternity Leave

I regret
that I could have done
so much more
these past three months

It is a tangible, physical feeling
caused by my fear, psychosis, and laziness
I see the regret on the furrow
accentuating Vaughan's tiny face
I see it in the teen acne
pocking my old slick face
I feel it in my rickety bones and
belly tires that rub up on one another
I see it behind late afternoon sitcoms
and early evening wine
I see it in my frustrated fingers vibrating from
their misuse and unspent ideas
I hear it in his frustrated cries
begging for stimulation
but worst of all

I see it in the clock
that has stolen away
never to return

The Ramp

South of this simply stacked city
the smoke bellows
horizontal white smoke
ushered along
by a day wind
deep and cello-like
taking with it
leaves, napkins and
various edges of the city

An unidentifiable object
makes a random guttural sound
unrelated and periodic
with of each gust
so I turn my ears off
still the sound bends me to
its general direction

I can see home from here
across the bay with its
angry whitecaps
a clean distance
free of fog
I feel my son's infant feet
cold and protruding from his sleep nest
inside he is warm and content
cooing and softly moaning in sleep

On the rusty deck of an afternoon bar
small marina boats rise slowly in
this corner of the bay
where I know we are safe and
close to my husband's work
my wine is still well above the
half way mark and my societal job
is months away
and we three
are stitched
and tattooed
by name

Fear Of Time

My child and I are natal warriors
untied by time
our private moments
strung between our eyes
a tightrope of promises
whispered and guard-less
a never ending bond
in jagged nights
softened by darkness
where we touch
constructed with sealed skin

The Last Song To Be Played At My Funeral

Drinking tepid mist
rising from inside
lapping at the surface
always there
a deep sea dysfunction
a dying octopus
wrapping its tentacles
tight
around
inserting
inside
grey organs left for the needle
leaving me gasping
this is all I know:
thick digits
plump sausages
speckled salt fish
tongue slapping
spring cheeks with
an autumn mold
yet to arrive
how we fight for what we think we need

Birthday Poem

Where I have done my darkest work
hid well beneath stretch marks
and panties and cuts and
scars and skirts and
bruises and lies and
knee socks and fat and dated tees
from concerts I no longer remember

I am wife beaters mismatched in black shades
stretched over one another and mis-sewn
I am rain boots fastened with glue, sounding
a ticktock meter against the ground
I am desert and ocean
I am disgusting and wholesome
I am a sustaining smile, wobbling
beneath a quilt fashioned against
the shallowest part of my birth skin

Still, I breathe

Question the obvious that
detracts from the exposed pink muscle
dissected and stretched on black auger
a crucified amphibian
scientific layers pinned as
silent as a decomposed and
mouth raped jesus that lies
rotting under a Fresno sun

his last bead of sweat
spat from his breast
the word of the lord

Still. I breathe.

The Abundant Affliction

Her fear the heart of a deer
Snow White, born from a drop of blood
once let onto the pure white snow

She knew what she was getting herself into
as her lips, young as red inviting tulips
pressed down upon the thick ripe apple
breath by breath
she suffocated death
from under the urn of glass

At attempt of three
Sylvia turned up the dial
till she could no longer see
blank pages ghostly as sheeted snow
flutter pressed against kitchen windows
like a flock of lost moths
in a miniature winter storm
set behind closed doors
she crawled into her gassy coffin

Legends collide with one hot breath
two mouths damp with desperation
gasping for that fine line between
pulse and persecution
as they rolled over to the warmth
of ancestors come to get them

My mortal choice has been stolen
by someone the size of a cherry tomato
who is replacing my human form with history
a shape shifter living off me like
a raw animal, bound and kept
by a thin envelope of skin and placenta

My ears have become razors whose enemies
quiver upon the lips of darkness like
a thousand gulls flocked
in ravenous desperation, their piercing cries
dancing deep upon the string of my spine

My nose an awkward gaping tunnel
inhaling distant dinners with bionic fever
meaty molecules rape nasal stalactites
that weep like swollen udders
their pustuled tips groan
for input that pleases
and search for salivating mammals
encroaching upon
my territory
in search of my young

My breasts engorged useless fruits
pounding their way out
with phantom knuckles and fists
pendulous sacks of hot wet sand
thick with unspent nectar
rotting on the wicked vine
begging for release

My stomach
a den of thieves
pilfers rubbish fit for beggars
squirreling morsels away
for someone else's pleasure
only to have it sent back up hot and fetid
thrown upon my tongue like a spoiled diner
hurling the finest caviar
across this bistro of perfection
created for its bidding

I limp about a sore sack of rot
a backdrop of moods
host to the regret
that 'fucking' brought
to this once barren ground
of my gaping loin
no longer privy to
Snow White's poisoned apple
or Sylvia's suicidal oven

The remainder of my carcass
will be left for the mortician
who will harvest my body
for what can be trimmed
pinned photographed and
propped up as a human mom

Bedding Down With A City

When the city slowly sighs
at the five o'clock hour
she becomes an entirely different beast.

A beast of glory and sauntering persuasion
a beast who lets you cum in her mouth and
sleep well past noon... in 'her' bed.

She won't ask you for your number or
drag you out to the local walk - of - shame for breakfast.
In fact, she'll even wait until after you've gone
before she strips the well-worn sheets
from the sweaty night bed.

If you make the mistake of offending her
asking for her facebook name
crapping in her toilet without a courtesy flush
not asking when using her toothbrush or
letting the 'L-word' slip.
You know.

Stuff like that.
She'll let it slide.

Because she's cool like that.
cool like silk in the palm
like aged whiskey

like perfectly tuned jazz
early on a Sunday afternoon
like the smell of your first kiss
like the sight of the exact person
you want to see
at that second.

She is cool like that, San Francisco.

She is a beautiful beast
with secrets seeping from her concrete hair
that flows from salty shores to
shallow muddy bay.

She has a million lovers.

If you are graced enough to become one
treat her like the beast she is
take her down like Santo Amor on a
thick sultry bed of urban desire
and drive it down her narrow avenues
all night long.

Don't forget the courtesy flush.

Mojave

Weep the Mojave of our lives
intertwined
will be measured by footprints of the godless
howled away by monsoon winds
hours before the scientist can observe, squint and collect
the awkward miles between our chase.

We are a step ahead
a step behind
we are a break-up ahead
a heartbreak behind

We are crying and sick
forgotten by one another
deep within the molded pages of
schoolroom nap books
dog-eared, mucoused, spat upon twice

We are metered by liquids
with solids and in-between space
our eyes cross while driving the freeway
locomotion matching speed, side by side

Wide trees stand still
we have crossed the globe and back again
without the notice of the clock tower
that bends over backward in travel

Morro Bay

Our toes curl around losing sand
we can see a tomorrow from here
while pulling in eel and shark
puffer fish and urchin and all blends
sea stuffs that sully the
catacombed bay

It feels good to have the shore under my feet
something besides asphalt and city
we are not real in the world of
labels and jars and bandages
held wobbly with paper doll arms
folded at the pulpy dashed seams

Waters swarm a craggy, coastal rock
sea stars sieve unwanted fragments of
remorse, sea beard, and seal fur collected
from an overgrown season of tides
we shore shepherds sink slowly
categorizing the kept and the cast:

Reset button of smooth, brown curled shell –kept
Second chance bit of dry urchin dome –kept
Found fears sea salt rust –cast

Our toes curl around losing sand
we can see tomorrow from here

pulling in eel and shark
puffer fish and urchin
sea stuffs that sully the
marrow of the bay

Don't Take It Home

Don't take it home
don't carry that unfinished baggage
across the threshold of marital bliss
dangling participles grinding and
bleeding on the doorstep
trailing on the freshly vacuumed rugs
and swept floors
waiting for your devoted feet

Don't take it home
don't bring it
to the dinner table
a dripping bag of unfinished business
to the marital mattress
like an unintentional dessert
gone screaming
against the stark white ceiling

Don't take it home
don't stock up on unspent
orgasm before the sun rises
on the return flight

To let it out on damp grass
in a stone walled yard
let the little beast free
to the running water

the open wanting drain
cold tiles, pressed nipples
body quietly shifting

Mouth silenced
under footsteps above
rousting around
they who do not care

Spent deaths down the drain

Trouble

I'm in trouble with the law again
the wild rider who runs my dreams
has tracked a trail of day old blood
and rotten thoughts of masturbating
with my shampoo bottle

These are nights when I bed down
with the drunk of myself who
bumps in the night fighting
stability with a sharp stick
and an empty smashed glass

My frontal lobe sifts through
daily fibers of pregnancy tests
tampons' plastic sheaths
a walk by the bay with Karl
and visual snips I stole
with no words

The crumbs lace digits with
dictionaries of discarded worries
stored in the creases of a knitted brow
to create a dialogue with rolling eyes
and deep, longing breaths

That drive me vertical in the dark
clapping against the empty air

and yelling in silence
attempting to drive away the stranger
who sneaks into my home at night

Oakland

I don't like her
I don't love her
I hella love her
I hella love
Oakland

I hella love her crust, rough around the peel
a burnt onion sweet to the center
each luscious layer a different taste

I love her parking god, lording over
a kingdom of empty spaces
meters ticking at an hour to the quarter

I love the tidy bicycle gangs
boys in pressed white tees, rolling out like
freeway dashes dotting down International avenue

I love my crackhead neighbor who
swears he's clean, hand-in-hand with Jesus
sings throat cancer with open hands
and surprises our front lawn
with a mower and a cigarette
on early Saturday mornings

I love the hipster city folk, little
trailing ants from across the bay

turning Oakland into the discovery channel
bar on BART
un-gated dispensaries
at your service

I love Doris and her dead husband, Earl
a year in the ground now, suits still closeted
empty cases of two buck chuck pillar their porch

I love my dad, as dead as Earl
who brought me here, heels dragging
from the shores of that urban Disneyland

I love my rock solid home and backyard stage
windows unbarred, silver and open
overlooking the silhouette from where I have come

I love my
"I Hella (heart) Oakland" tee
once a novelty, now chesting it
with well-earned pride

I love the SS Corman-Roberts and their captain
Paul who huffed life back into
my sad and brittle corpse
taught me how to slip my hand
inside this town

I hella love Mr. VanKleef, Mr. Heinold and
the 2101 Club - wine in fairy sized bottles
third one's on the house

I hella love Oakland
and I think maybe
just maybe
she hella loves me too

Naked In A Morgue

Times like this
under the breath of
sticky black scalpel
hovering just so above
Sir Embalmer's
tight-lipped canvas
cold to the touch

Times like this
we are left
in waiting rooms
hard-clutched with
skin chaffed to worry

Hair follicles pucker
fingernails quicken
in one last dance
of the body's
earthly facilities

Times like this
we are left
of center
under the care
of crisp blades

Painless to the touch
bloodletting plump
pale second-hand thighs
spread like a frog
under the will
of death

Popularity

I am voted most likely, one out of three
to commit suicide or at least make
a grand attempt
but it is here, in silence and forest and
wind fluffing a tree-lined frame
for Half Dome and Bridal Veil falls
that I can safely crawl back to
the security of my impending death –
old age, breast cancer, the 38 Geary

Come at me with a vengeance
you grim-reaping
motherfuckers

San Francisco

You fucking little slut

I was the only one
that's what you told me
during our long walks in the park
late nights in North Beach
Sundays on the Bay
watching the normals walk dogs
and run for health
while we kicked back the last
champagne and Four Loco

Now you little slut
you spread 'em for another
one after another, after another
tens and hundreds and
god knows, maybe thousands

San Francisco
you little slut

Your thighs chaffed at the 101 and 280 split where
trains and Giants fans
fight for a piece of your precious flesh
strangers
touching you and rubbing you and
trying to stay the night

"It's too late to catch the BART..."

Wah
You
Little
Slut

Little hipster ants running
back and forth
and back and
forth and back
and
forth
over
the 16th and Valencia G spot

Last I heard you're even letting Google buses
cum inside of you
without a condom
his insides spilling into your
deep dark places
changing your DNA
becoming more him than you

Even the Guardian is ruined

Once reserved for poets and the poor
now a couple grand in the back pocket of
Sir Papa Landlord
will grease the foundation springs
that keep City Hall afloat

Oh

San Francisco
you little slut
your head in Marin
one hand in the Pacific
the other in Oakland
gateway to jesus
dissected by midwestern mosquitos

I'll hold your hand when you die
while the ants trail from the ventricles
of your heart and
into the bigger parts of another town
blood gushing from the new
baby bridge pipes decorated with technology
feeding your nemeses with X's

Some day
you will hurt
like I do

From my Fruitvale perch I
watch your busty bridges heave
their last pathetic sigh

I will
miss you
in a stalker kind of way
a love gone sour
a full house of high school polaroids

Because

Some day the Google buses will
have rusted and leave you with
a cunt full of tetanus
his aged semen will
wither upon your clit
where the ants have left a pile of empty eggs
and torn the plaids in strips
in an attempt to wipe away the proof
that you San Francisco
are a slutty lover
who obviously lets
anyone in
for the right price

ABOUT THE AUTHOR

Missy Church is the author of a dozen chapbooks, four of which were featured in City Lights Books. Her works include *Zymosis, Balm of Inception, The Third Rail,* and *Stealing Spiders.*

Missy lives in Fruitvale, Oakland with her family and the creative remains of animal parts stored in glass jars.

She hosts *Naked Bulb*, an open mic, in her back yard, every third Saturday.

Missy is active in her community and, together with her group of literary friends, brought *Beast Crawl* to life. It is the first large-scale poetry festival for Oakland and the East Bay.

Find more at
missychurchwrites.tumblr.com

More
Paper Press
Books

Murder – Michael Rothenberg
Poems About Something and Nothing – Karl Kempton
Death At Sea – Youssef Alaoui
Notes From An Orgy – Paul Corman Roberts
Cineplex – Dennis Formento
Mrs. Jones Will Now Know – El Habib Louai
Lost Frames Compendium – Youssef Alaoui, Ed.

Made in the USA
Charleston, SC
03 August 2016